T0082774

GET YOUR
S.H.I.T.
TOGETHER

SELF-CARE, HAPPINESS, INNER PEACE AND TIME

CRYSTAL ROSE

GET YOUR S.H.I.T. TOGETHER
SELF-CARE, HAPPINESS, INNER PEACE AND TIME

iUniverse books may be ordered through booksellers or by contacting:

iUniverse
1663 Liberty Drive
Bloomington, IN 47403
www.iuniverse.com
844-349-9409

Because of the dynamic nature of the Internet, any web addresses or links contained in this book may have changed since publication and may no longer be valid. The views expressed in this work are solely those of the author and do not necessarily reflect the views of the publisher, and the publisher hereby disclaims any responsibility for them.

Any people depicted in stock imagery provided by Getty Images are models, and such images are being used for illustrative purposes only.
Certain stock imagery © Getty Images.

ISBN: 978-1-6632-1140-8 (sc)
ISBN: 978-1-6632-1141-5 (e)

Print information available on the last page.

iUniverse rev. date: 10/27/2020

CONTENTS

INTRODUCTION

What we consider as getting our life together is a psychological drive to attaining the state of being totally satisfied and happy within ourselves. Since we all are imperfect, we can't direct our lives to perfection and wipe out every bit of chaos that we face. So, we as human beings cannot be totally satisfied ever. Yet, what we can do is minimize the mess in our life with slight adjustments in our behavior and approach to everyday mannerisms.

When chaos occurs, you are always left off balance but there are only a few who pick themselves up before it's too late. There are those who are left wondering how they ended up in the situation or how they will move on. Whilst time doesn't wait for them and boom, it's been years and you are still disheveled. Why does it happen that way! Sometimes controlling our life could be very difficult but it is not impossible. What you rather need is to be strong emotionally to keep yourself away from all the negativity that your mind takes in and/or reacts upon and keep moving forward. This way you will be in a happier place.

Multiple aspects contribute to happiness and you cannot possibly expect to fix every aspect in just a day or two. An effective approach is to control things one after the other.

In this book, I will not only outline measures you can use to get your life together but also explain in detail how. If you therefore follow this plan, I promise you a journey where you will discover that it's not hard to find meaning and become happier in your daily routine.

MY STORY

I never imagined my life would be the way it is today. Coming from a girl who was broken, lost and disconcerted, I have come a long way. Rewinding my adolescence years, I had a different perspective on life at a young age. I knew life was hard based on my environment, but I never really understood why. Going through so many changes as a young woman I had so many questions, but I never really had anyone to provide answers to them.

Due to the condition that I had no one to really answer my questions I basically tried to figure it out on my own. You're probably saying in your mind "well, why didn't you ask for help?" See, some people aren't good at asking for help because they are used to being the helper. That was me! By this point I had experienced an imbalance of give and take. Through the years of trying to figure it out on my own I made mistakes which drove me into a deeper hole of being broken and lost. I didn't love myself and I didn't feel loved. I battled with insecurities. I would look for love in all the wrong places, but I didn't know I was only digging a deeper hole for myself. All I knew was, I had all this love inside of me; I just wanted to give and receive love.

It took me some time from experiences to learn that not everyone has the same heart as you much less think like you. I was hurt, betrayed and misunderstood by many. The more I became hurt, misunderstood and betrayed I turned cold.

After my first year in college I had my son and that was the first time in a long time I felt love. I had someone who loves me unconditionally and at that time it was the best feeling in the world. Still is!

When my son was born, I would always think and say to myself, "I need to figure out a way to provide the best life I can for him". I didn't want him to grow up and go through the things I did or feel the way I did. Even though having my son was the best thing to have happened to me I still suffered from past traumas.

It was a struggle being a single mom and dealing with past traumas. I was unhappy, I cried out of nowhere sometimes and I even thought about taking my life at one point because I didn't know how I could possibly be the best mom to my child. I found myself breaking down more and more stressed out because I was a struggling mom. I was working almost every day and at one point, I would say I feel like I'm working for nothing because I didn't see my paycheck. It went all to my bills. I was a struggling single mother; I didn't qualify for welfare because I made a couple dollars over the income ratio. There were times when I would scoop change out my wallet and car just to have enough for lunch at work. And on some days I'd go without having lunch. I stretched every dollar. I was becoming frustrated by the day, and in weeks and couple of months, I felt alone, and lost. I had no clue what I could do anymore.

Before my grandmother passed, she will always tell me to pray on things. I would pray to God, but I didn't think my prayers were being answered. I found myself losing hope about everything and even daily life. The stress became worst. I would get this burning sensation on the top of my head to the point hair started falling out, I couldn't sleep at night, and during the day I really didn't have the energy to do the things that I needed to do. I was having anxiety attacks and ended up in the emergency room.

One day I became overwhelmed everything was in turmoil I couldn't help it; I broke down. I was on my knees, face buried in my hands crying and conversing with God all at the same time. I just had to let out every emotion and thoughts I was feeling. I had to go see a doctor and that was when I found out that what I was going through was really depression. The doctor prescribed me pills so that it'll help ease my mind and so I could sleep well at night.

I was never too fond about taking pills, but there was one day I just couldn't sleep: my mind was racing with all these thoughts, so, I decided to take the pill. The next day I woke up I just didn't feel right. It's like all my thoughts had vanished — I felt like an air head to the point I had to call out of work. I dropped my son off to school that morning, but I went back home and just sat there. There were no thoughts in my head at all. I tried going out to get some fresh air in hopes I would feel better by the time my son got out of school. So, I drove to the house of my son's grandmother. It was down the street from his school. I could barely make it up her steps. I just sat there staring into space with no thoughts in my head. Thank goodness for my son's grandma; she was able to pick him up because I was just all the way off.

Later, that same day, the medication I had taken started to wane off.

Slowly my thoughts were coming back and all I can say is I didn't feel right. When my senses came about, I promised myself I will never take that pill again. I wouldn't wish that feeling upon no one, not even my worst enemy. I knew I had to get my shit together so I can be the best person I can be especially, for my son who depended on me. From that day forward I took accountability and worked on, getting my shit together. It's not an easy journey, but I'll be damned to go back down that road again.

After being diagnosed I tried so much. Every day after that was a constant battle. I was fighting each and every day — I still am. After doing my research on depression, I understood that depression never really goes away, but how I chose to cope with it determined the life I live. I knew that it could either make me or break me. Being depressed will not get me the life I knew I wanted to live, and of course, create for my son.

I decided to try counseling, but after a few sessions I realized I needed to help myself. I didn't rely on medication or a counselor, but me! When I came to that conclusion I didn't know how I was going to do it. It needed to be done as I was determined. Counseling was not a bad thing, however I had felt like I needed to do this on my own. One thing that stuck with me from attending counseling sessions was the fact that I had to learn to make myself a priority. Once I drilled that into my head I started to research and took every necessary action.

I was always working and when I was not working, I'm

attending to my son as I should. Every day was the same routine for me. Making myself a priority, I needed to break that routine. I started spending time alone after my son went to bed or when he was with his grandma. I would read, go for coffee, and take walks to be attuned with nature. Those were a few things I always enjoyed doing, but drifted away from due to my circumstances. Being alone, I started talking to myself and I felt good because I was getting to know myself. It's okay to talk to yourself; "it doesn't mean you are crazy."

Talking to myself had now become a part of my daily routine. Daily, I had to check in with myself, "Crystal, how are you doing today? Are you happy?" Asking myself those questions brought awareness to how I felt and helped me set the mood for my day. If the answer was negative, I would turn it into a positive one. I embraced positivity, even if that meant singing "every little thing is gonna be alright" by Bob Marley. Beautifully, that song has gotten me through some stressful times.

Making myself a priority and checking in was necessary because being a work in progress, I was at the vulnerable edge of easily slipping into being depressed. To prevent myself from feeling depressed, I had to do what was necessary for me to keep the peace I was seeking and found within myself. I turned my focus on solely getting to know and love myself. I learned that I was gullible. I couldn't be that anymore, so I walked away from everything and everyone that negatively impacted my life — That included old habits as well. I stopped giving access to unnecessary things that take away the essence from my peace.

It's okay to let go of certain things, people and environments that no longer align with your purpose. I started channeling my energy to the things that gave me power and did not make me powerless. I could have never healed by holding on to the things I needed to let go of or the trauma which kept me in the past.

When the wrong people and things leave your life, better things start to happen for your life. People will lie, hate and quit on you, but you have to make sure you don't quit on yourself. I was done with running from my problems and most of all running from myself. I had to be okay with admitting to myself that I'm not okay and start living in my truth. Everything I was going through in life was meant to build me up and not break me. Yes, I may have struggles, but you can never make your struggles let you think life is over. Good news: It is not over. I had to step up and be the person I'm destined to be. I set the tone for my life, therefore, I had to get my S.H.I.T together.

SKIN CARE

It all starts with skin care, which is important because your skin is the greatest barrier against all things when it comes to your body. Being depressed, I didn't care about my skin as much I should. I washed my face, sometimes put on a little foundation and went about my day. I used to hate looking at myself in the mirror, but one day I went to work, and my coworker said, "girl did you sleep last night?" At that moment I got up from the desk, went to the bathroom and I looked in the mirror. I noticed the bags under my eyes, a few blemishes and my skin was not radiant. I was not pleased at how I looked and from that day I told myself I have to take better care of my skin. All I can think of is that what I'm feeling on the inside is starting to show on the outside. What we fail to realize is that depression can also lead to other sicknesses. Therefore, taking care of your health should be essential.

So, I developed a skin care routine for myself night and day: I would get up early, do my skincare routine and shower before I woke my son up, and prepared him for school. Just by having that 'alone time' in the morning helped me prepare properly for my day. I felt refreshed and rejuvenated each time I did my skin care routine. I started to notice how good I felt and became consistent with it. I believe skin care plays a big part in your self-care routine because you certainly don't want to look like what you been through; much less look like what you're going through. I can't stress it enough how important skin care is, especially for us woman we like to have smooth, soft skin that radiates. I like to look at skincare as transforming, being that your skin is shedding skin cells throughout the day. Each day you put time and effort into taking care of your skin your making progress. Accept your transformation as long as it reflects your progression.

Starting a skincare routine has significantly helped my depression and I've read a lot of you revealing the same thing. I want to talk about it!

For me, it has given me something to look forward to when I get out of bed, and something to look forward to throughout the day. It's a huge distraction from thinking negative thoughts, and I've been really encouraged by seeing positive results when adding in a new technique. The ritual of practicing a physical kind of self-care has also improved the way I feel about myself. Unfortunately, anxiety and depression are commonplace. And many in the medical community believe the number of people affected is increasing.

If you don't suffer from a mental or emotional condition yourself, it's likely that someone in your family does; Or someone in your social circle.

According to the Anxiety and Depression Association, 40 million U.S. adults suffer from an anxiety disorder. That's 18% of the population!

Did you know that a skin care routine can help manage depression and anxiety?

It's Not Just About Beauty

I'm not talking about looking younger or more attractive. Even though good skin care definitely does that, I want to talk about the psychological benefits of a daily skin care ritual. Specifically, I'm talking of how it can help you manage anxiety and depression.

Let's explore why a skin care routine is so valuable for people who struggle with mental and emotional conditions.

The Magic of a Daily Routine

Mental health professionals encourage their patients to establish healthy, daily routines. These include exercise, proper meditation, eating nutritious meals at specific times every day, And maintaining a consistent sleep schedule.

There are several reasons for this — Anxiety and depressions make you feel out of control. A routine helps you regain a sense of control and empowerment. Your life feels more manageable. This, in turn helps you build self-confidence.

Stress Management

Anxiety and depression put our brains on stress overload. However, daily routines give our brains a rest.

A woman interviewed for an article entitled "Can Skincare Keep You Sane" explained that following a daily skin care regimen helps her more than weeks of counseling sessions. It shortens the duration of her depressive episodes and empowers her to take control of her emotional well-being.

Women who have a skin care ritual credit it for giving them a positive start to their day. At night, it helps them calm down and ease their mind from the stressof the day.

Focusing on a soothing skin care routine can help the brain get out of negative thought patterns. Applying serums, creams, and cleansers activates several senses and gives the mind something positive to focus on.

Which Products Are Best?

Want to start a daily skin care routine to help manage your mental and emotional challenges? You are probably wondering what type of products to use.

Funny you should ask...

Seek the very best ingredients for your precious skin. It's a conscious choice to prioritize product quality.

Life is hard enough; Don't be hard on your skin. Toxins have no place in healthy skin self-care. Your skin will absorb them and negate the benefits of the ritual. And they can put you at risk of additional health issues such as cancer or organ toxicity. They can even alter your reproductive system. Pair one of these scary diseases with depression and you'll have a truly monstrous health threat!

Self-Nurturing Increases Quality of Life

Think nourishment. Think soothing fragrances. Think silky and smooth to the touch. Gently massage your face and get that dopamine pumping;Vitamin and mineral-rich super fruits feed your skin — They support emotional well-being and balance. Unbelievably high antioxidant levels combat the free radicals that threaten your health. Remember that anxiety and depression can weaken your immunity. There are aromatherapy benefits from the gorgeous essential oil and fruit fragrances.

An Additional Tool For Anxiety and Depression Management

Clinical depression and anxiety are complex conditions. I'm not suggesting that a skin care routine alone is sufficient. However, many people maintain a daily skin care routine to help manage their mental health challenges. Regardless of your specific health issues—taking care of yourself is essential. We all deserve that, right?

HAPPINESS

When I was going through my depression phase, I couldn't see much less feel what happiness was. Besides my son, I did not know what truly made me happy. I asked myself several times what makes you happy and I couldn't answer the question. I was out of touch with my happiness.

For years I spent searching outside of myself for answers that always resided in me. I knew that if I wanted to come up out of this depression and know what makes me happy, I had to take accountability and dig a little deeper. Have you ever had a feeling come over you where you just feel fulfilled? You can't help but, smile because life is so good. That's what happiness looks and feels like. Happiness is a choice and it's up to you to intentionally choose it. Take responsibility of that peace and joy that lives inside of your heart and own your happiness because no one can make you happy, but you. Even though life is challenging, rough and you may get discouraged, keep in my mind that you grow through what you go through. You are not a product of your past and you are not a product of your environment or your current situation, but you are a product of how you navigate your life's storm.

Do what truly makes you happy! Doing what truly makes you happy will attract more to be happy about. The positive energy you put out by doing the things that make you happy attracts more positive energy back to you, so, it only makes sense to eliminate or reduce anything that makes you unhappy. Anything that gives you negative energy should be replaced with more of the things that makes you feel alive and joyful. Yes, we may have people in our lives that makes us happy, but we shouldn't solely depend on them making you happy, they should only add to your happiness. See, you have to ask yourself what you want out of life. You need to know and be exact about it because until then will you know when you have happiness. Don't be vague and say "oh I just want to be happy!" You really need to know; really need to feel it on the inside. Once you know what you want and it brings you joy, you'll start to see how it reflects in all aspects of your life. You'll feel good about yourself and as you feel better about yourself, you'll treat yourself better.

Remember you are entitled to a great life; take responsibility for your own happiness. In order to get there, visualize yourself being happy. There will be times when things will not go right, but, you have to see beyond your circumstances. Choose to see the good, the lesson and the blessing in everything. Live the way you want; follow your intuition and not feel guilty about doing things your way. Take care of yourself, your mental, spiritual and physical health.

Getting things is not going to make you happy. Whether it be money, material things, relationships, and opportunities: All those things will only make you happy for the moment. Those things will always change; life is always changing no matter what you do. You don't have to work at changing yourself because change is going to happen automatically. The real key is progress. You have to grow and make progress, because your progress equals happiness. You have to take control of this process and own your own happiness.

Happiness is life's most desired goal. However we can never achieve it while we continue to look outside of ourselves, as it is an inside job.

"Happiness cannot be travelled to, owned, earned, worn or consumed. Happiness is the spiritual experience of living every minute with love, grace, and gratitude". — Anonymous Throughout our evolutionary journey we have tried every strategy imaginable and searched almost everywhere in our quest for true happiness. We have had some great experiences and learnt a lot along the way, but we have never found what we are searching for. Eventually, we grow tired of searching and turn our attention to the one place we haven't looked so far; inside ourselves. True happiness is not something that can be sought and acquired; it is our soul's natural state of being, and one we can only connect with by going within.

Anything we do, it is simply our inner quality that we are going to spread. We cannot do anything of tremendous value for our planet until anything of accurate value occurs within us. Thus, if we want to be connected to the world, the first thing we must do is to transform ourselves right into happy beings.

It doesn't matter what we do in our life, whether it is business, studying or giving assistance to someone or some cause, we're doing it because deep down, it gives us satisfaction. Each activity that every individual executes on this globe rises from a desire. We were not unhappy when we were a child, as joy and happiness is a source which resides within each one of us. So all we have to do is to go for it and take charge of that joy which is residing in us. Everything in universe is in order. The sun comes wonderfully well up in the sky. The flowers flourish beautifully, no stars falls along, and the galaxies are functioning perfectly. Today, the whole cosmos is occurring divinely well, but just a negative thought warming up on our brain enables us to believe that today is a poor day.

Suffering occurs basically when most human beings carry a perception as regards what this life is all about. Our emotional process becomes far larger than the existential procedure, or our petty creation becomes far more critical, compared to GOD's Creations, to place it bluntly. This is the way to obtain all suffering. We miss the complete sense of what this means to be alive here. An emotion within us or a thought within our mind establishes the nature of the experience right now. Our thoughts may have nothing to accomplish even with the restricted reality of our lifestyle. The entire creation is happening beautifully well but just one considered emotion may ruin everything. Anything we consider as "our mind" isn't ours basically; It is merely society's empty talk. Everyone and anyone whom we encounter on a daily basis put some idea or information in our head and we truly have no choice about whose idea we accept or don't. This information is advantageous once we learn HOW TO process them and use them. This accumulation of opinions and information that we collect is simply useful for our survival in this world. It is not something which is related to who we are.

First thing we need to do in the morning when we get up is to smile.

At whom? No one! Since just the fact that we have woken up is not a small matter. Thousands of people who slept yesterday evening didn't wake up today. Isn't it great that we woke up? So, look as you wake up; look around you if there is someone, and then smile at them. As this morning, for numerous people, someone precious to them didn't get up. Venture out, take a deep breath and look at the bushes. They didn't die yesterday either.

You may think this is really funny, but you won't know its reality until someone dear to you doesn't wakeup. So don't wait until you understand the value of it. Appreciate what you have, be happy that you are alive and everyone who matters to you is still around.

Of course, people who do not have food or the basic needs for living can feel physically miserable and their needs must be addressed. Our duty as a human being is to help and take care of such people when we encounter them. But most people are unhappy not as a result of what they don't have. It is because they compare their life to others. You are driving on a motorbike, you see somebody cruising in a Mercedes and you suddenly become unhappy. But you wouldn't know that for someone who is driving a bicycle, your motorbike seems like a limousine.

Life is about learning and appreciating what GOD has created for us on this planet. It is not about twisting and distorting it. When we rely on external situations to make us joyful and contented, we will never feel true happiness. The quality of our life doesn't depend on what car we drive, how much money we have in a bank account, or how big our house is, but how content and happy we feel inside.

Although each one of us is unique, and what works for one may not for the other, but there are simply areas that tend to make a big difference to people's happiness in life. Crucially, they are all areas that are within our control:

1. Care for others genuinely: Caring genuinely for others around us is essential to our happiness. Being caring means wishing the best for others, and acknowledging in them the same wants, needs, aspirations, and even fears that we have too. It means providing a listening ear, noticing when someone needs help, and helping our community without asking for a reward. Being caring allows us to have empathy for others and to live a life based on affection, love, and compassion for the people around us.

2. Connect with people: "Happiness is influenced not only by the people you know, but by the people they know". This means that by surrounding ourselves with happier people we become happier, we make the people close to us happier, and make the people close to them happier. People with strong and vast social relationships are happier, healthier and live longer. Close relationships with family and friends brings love, compassion, meaning and belonging into our lives and grow our sense of self-worth.

"To touch the soul of another human being is to walk on holy ground" — Stephen Covey

3. Notice the world around you: Taking notice is about observing those things that we find beautiful and being mindful of them in our daily life. It can be easy to rush through life without stopping to notice much. Paying more attention to the present moment, to our own thoughts and feelings, and to the world around us; can improve our wellbeing. Becoming more aware of the present moment not only help us to enjoy the world around us more and understand ourselves better, but also recognize things that we have been taking for granted.

4. Have something to look forward to: Happiness in anticipation is the key here. By having something to look forward to, no matter how our situations, bring happiness into our life —well before the circumstance happen. If your life is a series of undesirable duties, commitments, and unpleasant tasks; take some time to find out something that YOU would find enjoyable and make time to do it. "Our authentic happiness is blocked by our false belief that life should be how we want it to be. The expectation that accompanies this false belief sets us up for disappointment, frustration, anger and unhappiness". Our expectations create our reality and they change our lives emotionally and physically. Unreasonable expectations can make life extremely hard and unhappy. These expectations are actually designed by our ego, as nothing give our ego a stronger sense of self-identity as an experience that supports our sad life-story. "In other words, we unconsciously create expectations so we can feel sad and disappointed when they

are not met. Our ego is addicted to sadness and painful emotions". Master to drop all expectations and open your heart, begin to love yourself, and move beyond your ego. Embrace freedom from your ego.

"Happiness is the anticipation and the realization of the fulfilment of a dream." — Anonymous

5. Avoid false beliefs and expectations: Finding ourselves, our authenticity will help us to feel our beauty. When we endeavor to be who we are, to be true to ourselves, and accept ourselves with all our flaws and imperfections, we will automatically feel attractive and unique. Beauty is never dependent upon the approval of others. Quite the contrary, beauty is very much self-defined and self-created.

6. Be comfortable with who you are: "To be beautiful means to be yourself. You don't need to be accepted by others. You need to accept yourself." —Thich Nhat Hanh. By accepting ourselves and becoming kinder to ourselves we will be able to see our shortcomings as opportunities to learn and grow.

7. Find a purpose in life: We all have intact potential, perhaps even areas of intelligence, to become something entirely different, or somehow more than what we appear to be right now. People who find meaning and purpose in their lives are happier, feel more in control and get more out of what they do. They become less stressed, anxious, or depressed. How do we find meaning and purpose in life? We're all wired differently. Some of us feel more connected to nature, others find meaning by employing in nurturing. The key

is to know what works for us. Learning to live our purpose is essentially a spiritual exercise, and an inside job. Search how and what gives you that sense of fulfilment and deep connection; and then peruse it in all that you do.

8. Train yourself to be more positive: There is the positive aspect in everything, in every person, in every situation. Sometimes it's not obvious and we have to look hard. Even when we are faced with a difficult situation we can think to ourselves "What is good about this?" No matter how unpleasant the circumstance might look, we always can find something good if we take the time to think about it. Everything, good or bad is a learning experience. There is always lesson to be gained from every bad experience. "There are moments when troubles enter our lives and we can do nothing to avoid them. But they are there for a reason. Only when we have overcome them will we understand why they were there" — Paulo Coelho

9. Live Mindfully: "Life is not what it's supposed to be. It's what it is. The way you cope with it is what makes the difference" — Virginia Satir. Life is full of challenges. The way we manage them can make a difference between whether we let them control our lives, or we find a way to embrace every challenge as it arises. By practicing mindfulness, we can find a more empowering way to react to the challenges life brings us. It also helps us to train our mind, manage our thoughts and feelings, and reduce stress and anxiety.

10. Take care of your body: "Your body is precious. It is our vehicle for awakening. Treat it with care." —Buddha.

There is a powerful mind-body connection through which emotional, mental, social, spiritual, and behavioral factors can directly affect our health. Being active makes us happier as well as healthier. By spending time outdoors, eating healthy foods, and getting enough sleep, we can improve our wellbeing. A serene mind really is nothing without a healthy body to carry it, so show your body the same compassion that you show everyone, by taking care of it.

It is positively time now that we look inside of ourselves and see HOW TO produce personal wellbeing. From our own experience of life, we can clearly observe that wellbeing will come to us when we change our perception on life. We need to realize, if we are determined to create our happiness and wellbeing by the outside factors it will never happen. As nothing will be %100 the way we want them to be. When we accept this fact, we will be able to work on ourselves as individuals, to become the person we want to be. And happiness will be our only virtue which has been our authentic nature by creation in the first place.

"Focus on the journey, not the destination. Joy is found not in finishing an activity but in doing it." — Greg Anderson

INNER PEACE

Get Intune! Get Intune with being mentally and spiritually at peace. Having inner peace will eliminate stress, anxiety, fear, negative thoughts, emptiness and lack of satisfaction. We all battle with internal and external chaos. Life can be overwhelming and draining at times and it may seem hopeless to find silence and inner peace. I'll be honest; it takes inner strength to find and maintain inner peace. Inner peace is a choice and many of our habits determine how much peace you have in your daily lifestyle. You cannot win the war against the world if you can't win the war against your own mind. Change the way you think, you have to be prepared to accept the challenge.

We can reach peace in many ways by meditating, exercising, being in tuned with nature or simply just doing something you love that brings you peace. Radically, peace comes when we stop thinking or having thoughts which bother us. When our inner peace is disturbed, our inner clarity and in-born wisdom becomes distant and vague. When you start to feel like that you will most likely want to shift your focus way from clarity. Why not focus on the things you can control. Why worry about things you can't control? You have to know what you can control. If not, it'll bring more stress into your life. I used to worry over things which were out of my control. For example; what other people think about me or opinions they make of me.

After, numerous disagreements with family and friends, I came to the realization that I cannot change what people think. I had that "it is what is" attitude. While I developed that attitude, when certain situations came about, I was able to be at peace. I did not allow what people think, say, or do to interrupt my peace. You have to stop allowing the opinions of people who don't value you and what they think about you hold you back from breaking free. I had the understanding and knowledge to keep myself calm and strong during stressful times. Another important thing is learning to forgive. I didn't forgive because of them, but for myself. You should learn to forgive so that you can move forward and feel better. If you hold on to things, it'll only disturb your peace.

Also, you have to truly know yourself and what you are capable of. When you have inner peace, you fully accept yourself so you don't waste your energy, time and attention on meaningless thoughts. More peace will come consistently when what you think, feel, say and do are in alignment. Set limitations for yourself and don't make issues bigger than it is. When facing an issue that you think is major, ask yourself if the issue will still matter in 5 years. By answering this question, it'll help you look at the bigger picture. Sometimes we have to look deep within and let things go. One of my favorite reminders by John F. Kennedy is that "Peace is a daily, a monthly process, gradually changing opinions, slowly eroding old barriers, quietly building new structures."

With life always changing, we change and grow from what is happening. Life will either make us bitter, better or broken. Remember, peace means always choosing better. Just like happiness, peace is an inside job. Spending time on what's important to you and being true to yourself is the key to your inner peace. You'll never find inner peace until you listen to your heart. Trust me! Your heart knows best.

Inner peace is not something that just happens instantly the moment you choose you want it. The first step is to choose you want it though. Once you know you want it then you will be willing to commit the time and energy required in order to achieve it over time.

Inner peace is not easy, it will not come without work, but it will change your life for the better. If you follow the ten steps outlined below you will soon find yourself on the way to having greater inner peace and greater happiness and joy in all aspects of your life. It will take time, but these 10 ways to inner peace can get you there, if you are willing to let it happen.

Love

The first path to inner peace is to learn to love — Love others, and more importantly, love yourself. When you are able to open your heart to see the best in others and yourself you will start to realize that all of the minutia we sometimes focus on is irrelevant when the general beauty of the human people (and all life) far exceeds the perceived minor negatives we dwell on. So, open your heart and learn to give and receive love, it will bring you to inner peace.

Smile

The next key to inner peace is to smile. Smile when you are happy, smile when you are sad, smile when you do not feel like it. There is a power in smiling that is often overlooked. When you smile the odds of getting a smile back is greatly increased, and there are few things that help to give us more joy, and inner peace than having someone smile at us. We are wired to feel lighter and better when smiled at so why not choose to initiate it by choosing to smile, always, whenever and however you can.

Hug

The next step after learning to smile even when you don't feel like it is to reach out, offer and receive hugs. Shaking hands is nice but hugs are more powerful and beneficial to the giver and the receiver. Studies have shown that our physical and mental health are improved when we have an increase in physical contact with other people. 10 hugs a day should be your absolute minimum.

Forgive

This is a huge one, and often the step that most people get tripped up on. They find some weird pleasure in holding onto things that they don't want to forgive. Be it either the perceived control not forgiving gives them, or just the attention having a hurt can give them, they hold on. This does no one any good, especially the person who cannot forgive. If they cannot forgive others they will never be able to forgive themselves. And that is the biggest danger to inner peace — not being able to forgive one's self.

Serve

After you have taken the needed time to work on yourself and taken simple steps to both improve yourself and also learn to reach out to others, it will be time to take the next step. One of the hidden keys to inner peace is to learn to get out of our own ego and learn to put others first. This is where service can come in. It helps you to recognize that your stuff is minor compared to the stuff other people face every day. It also empowers you to understand that you have the power to enact change, even in simple ways, to help others to have a better life. This is very beneficial to your own inner peace.

Eat Well

You cannot have good mental health and inner peace if your physical body is out of shape. And the first place to address imbalance in the physical body is by looking at what you eat. This is a very challenging thing in our modern society because all of the cheapest, quickest and easiest to get foods are often the ones that are most detrimental to our health. Eat fruits and vegetables. Avoid fatty and or processed foods, the more natural it is, the better it is for you. This doesn't mean you shouldn't enjoy food; just be smart and don't take the easy way out with your food.

Do not numb yourself

This has become a very common problem in today's society. In order to truly achieve inner peace one must first be willing to honestly look at one's self and look for the areas which can be improved upon. Too often, people avoid this by numbing themselves in some manner. This could be numbing with alcohol or recreational drugs, or even prescription drugs, designed to help you not feel a thing at all. Other people numb themselves through seeing the TV or being addicted to other things such as sports, sex, etc. Do not get me wrong; I like all of the above, but there is a big difference between enjoying a nice scotch while you read versus drinking to no longer feel. Do not numb yourself. If you do, you will not not be able to achieve inner peace.

Stay Fit

This is the pair to eating healthy.Without a healthy physical body, the mental faculty will be in turmoil. When our bodies are not working because we have not put in the energy or the effort to keep them running well, the pain and discomfort we feel will distract us from being able to let go of things and allow inner peace to thrive. You do not have to be a gym rat, you just need to do something every day that will make you feel good, get your body moving, blood pumping and bring fresh air into your lungs. Just do something that gets you up and moving, no matter what it is.

Drink lots of H20 (water)

This is the hidden secret to inner peace. The most important thing you can do for yourself is to stay hydrated with good water. Do you have headaches? Probably dehydrated. Feel horrible when you wake up? Probably dehydrated. Find your mind isn't as sharp as it could be? Probably dehydrated. Drink more good water, you will be amazed the effect it has on you.

Meditate

This is the final and most crucial step to inner peace. If you really are looking to achieve inner peace, you have to learn how to slow your mind down. The simplest, cheapest and easiest way to slow your mind down is to sit quietly every day. I know this sounds all zen and possibly goofy, but don't think of men in saffron robes sitting around saying Oms, instead just sit and relax and focus on your breathing. Count your breath. It may take months of this to see a change, but when you hit that first fleeting moment of space between thoughts you will understand and be addicted.

Spend Time in Quiet Reflection

With all that's going on in the world today, one of the best things you can do to achieve inner peace is to minimize or eliminate reading newspapers and watching the news if you can. When we allow our mind to absorb the negativity that's around us, we become more detached from our spirituality and achieving inner peace.

When our mind has nothing to occupy it, it immediately feels insecure and looks for something to fill the void with. That's when we instantly turn on the TV or surf the internet; just anything to keep the mind busy.

Instead, when you find yourself with some free time, even if it's just 15 minutes, use that time to be still, to be by yourself, to focus inward. A guided meditation will help you take a huge leap forward toward inner peace.

You Are What You Think

We've been conditioned to think negativity — sad but true. People thrive on bad news; they buy it; they follow it; they seek it out. It's no wonder that so many people seem unhappy and withdrawn, unable to escape the self-imposed wall of negativity they've built around themselves.

We must take the necessary steps to avoid negative thinking. You'll never be able to achieve inner peace when you're focused on the negative.

There's simply nothing at all to be gained by thinking negative thoughts. Changing your way of thinking is not going to be easy — it doesn't happen overnight. But what steps are you willing to take to change your life and achieve inner peace?

You are the master of your mind, not the other way around. Take control of your thoughts and you'll not only take control of your life, but you'll achieve inner peace.

Simplify Your Life

"There's never enough time in the day."

How many times have you heard someone say that? We fill our days up with so many chores, tasks and mundane activities and as a result, we don't stand a chance in achieving inner peace. This is simply because we don't take the time.

You want to meditate but have to get the laundry done. You want to spend some time to yourself but the grass has to be mowed. You want to sit down for just a few minutes but you have to vacuum first.

When you stop placing demands on your time, you'll feel a weight lifted from your shoulders.

Prioritize your time by tackling the big tasks first, plan time for yourself, then accomplish some of the smaller tasks, but at a comfortable pace. You'll find your day a lot less hectic and a lot more enjoyable.

Quiet Time Alone Is The Foundation of Inner Peace

Each day we spend our time working for someone else, taking care of our families, cleaning, cooking, etc. Sadly, we never manage to find just 15 minutes to focus on inner peace.

Sitting quietly and simply listening to your breath allows the body and mind to relax.

This leads to inner peace. There's no amount of money that will bring you inner peace. There's nothing "without" you that can bring you inner peace. It must come from "within" you, from within those quiet moments of solitude when there is only you and stillness.

If you have trouble stilling your mind, ask your angels to help remove those busy thoughts so you can focus on your inner peace.

Be Immune to Flattery and Criticism

You must remember that it's not what others think, but what you think that matters.

We certainly can listen to the criticism and flattery of others, but if we depend on them, we rob ourselves of inner peace.

Allowing yourself to be affected by people who bestow either flattery or criticism on you will inflate your ego which pulls you further away from inner peace.

Allow yourself to have a strong sense of confidence and self. Know that your opinions are ultimately the ones that matter. Don't criticize anyone but instead accept them for who they are. Leave the criticism to those who lack good judgment and self-confidence.

Avoid Criticism of Others

It's vital that we empathize with others, to put ourselves in someone else's place.

We must be aware that everyone is fighting a battle of some kind. Criticism of others is a negative energy which deeply affects your sense of inner peace. When we criticize, it's impossible to feel inner peace. Instead, make a conscious effort to give your love and energy to others in need; and in doing so that positive energy will have a wonderful ripple effect.

This is not a get inner peace quick scheme. This will take time. This will take effort. But this will pay off in the end and you will find your inner peace growing and improving over time if you follow these 10 steps. You can do it; trust me; I believe in you. Just believe in yourself.

TIME

Our whole life revolves around time. Respect your time and understand the value of time because once time is gone you can't get it back. If you respect and understand the value of time it'll save you from so many regrets. You can't afford to waste time at all. Everything that was created by God has an expiration date. There is therefore, "A time to be born and time to do die." Valuing time should help you focus on what's important. Time is our only non-renewable resource. For instance, good health, your goals and dreams. If you value time it'll help you become productive and effective in your pursuit to your next level. Invest the greatest amount of time in yourself so you are rewarded with greatest pay off. You are your greatest investment.

I knew I wanted to be successful and in order for me to become successful I had to stop wasting my time on things that were distracting me and wasn't aligning with my success. When I stopped giving my energy and time to the wrong things my knowledge and experience sky rocketed. I became more productive and effective, utilizing my time wisely.

Once you learn to utilize your time correctly it will open up opportunities to success, sources of happiness, growth and prosperity and all the things we want. If you neglect time it can leave you with very little. Every morning you wake up you are living minutes that you can't back. There is no moment more important than right now. Not in a week, a month, or next year. Right now! The motive behind valuing your time is to maximize the moments of doing what you love and minimize the moments of doing what you don't. Allocate to the things that make you feel like today is powerful. There is no limitation. The only imitation is yourself.

Be picky with who you choose to spend your time with because you can't get that time back. The people in your life should be reducing stress not causing more of it. Choose those who fill you and those with positive energy. You are where you are because you decided to be. If you want change you have to manufacture change. Everything you every want is in front of you. Embrace it!

HOW YOU THINK and feel about yourself largely determines the quality of your life, and the emotional core of your personality is your self-esteem, defined as "how much you like yourself."

Your self-esteem is largely determined by the way you use your life and time in the development of your full potential. Your self-esteem increases when you are working efficiently, and your self-esteem goes down when you are not.

The flip side of the coin of self-esteem is called "self-efficacy," defined as the degree to which you feel you are competent, capable, and productive, able to solve your problems, do your work, and achieve your goals.

The more competent, capable, and productive you feel, the higher your self-esteem. The higher your self-esteem, the more productive and capable you will be. Each one supports and reinforces the other.

People who manage their time well feel positive, confident, and in charge of their lives.

THE PSYCHOLOGY OF TIME MANAGEMENT:

The Law of Control

The psychology of time management is based on a simple principle called 'The Law of Control'. This law states that you feel good about yourself to the degree to which you feel you are in control of your own life. This law also says that you feel negative about yourself to the degree to which you feel that you are not in control of your own life or work.

Psychologists refer to the difference between an internal locus of control, where you feel that you are the master of your own destiny, and an external locus of control, where you feel that you are controlled by circumstances outside yourself.

When you have an external locus of control, you feel that you are controlled by your boss and your bills, and by the pressure of your work and responsibilities. You feel that you have too much to do in too little time, and that you are not really in charge of your time and your life. Most of what you are doing, hour after hour, is reacting and responding to external events.

There is a big difference between action that is self-determined and goal-directed and reaction, which is an immediate response to external pressure. It's the difference between feeling positive and in control of your life and feeling negative, stressed, and pressured. To perform at your best, you must have a strong feeling of control in the important areas of your business and personal life.

Your Thoughts and Feelings

In psychological terms, each person has a self-concept; an internal master program that regulates his behavior in every important area of life. People with a high self-concept regarding time management see themselves and think about themselves as being well organized and productive. They are very much in charge of their lives and their work.

Your self-concept is made up of all of your ideas, pictures, images, and especially your beliefs about yourself, especially regarding the way you manage your time. Some people believe themselves to be extremely well organized and efficient. Others feel continuously overwhelmed by demands of other people and circumstances.

Beliefs Become Realities

What are your beliefs about yourself and your ability to manage your own time? Do you see yourself and think about yourself as a highly efficient and effective time manager? Do you believe you are highly productive and in complete control of your life and your work? Whatever your belief, if you think of yourself as an excellent time manager, you will naturally do those things that are consistent with that belief.

Because your self-concept causes you to continually strive for consistency between the person you see yourself as, on the inside, and the way you perform on the outside, if you believe you manage your time well, you will be a good time manager. You can take all of the courses on time management, read all the books, and practice the various systems, but if you perceive yourself as being a poor time manager, nothing will help. If you have developed the habit of being late for meetings and appointments, or you believe that you are a disorganized person, those habits become your automatic behavior. If you do not change your beliefs about your personal levels of effectiveness and efficiency, your ability to manage your time will not change, either.

Make a Decision

How do you develop new, positive beliefs about yourself and your level of personal productivity? Fortunately, it is not difficult. You simply use the four Ds: desire, decisiveness, determination, and discipline. Most importantly, make a decision to develop a specific time management habit, like being early for every meeting for the unforseeable future. Every change in your life comes about when you make a clear, unequivocal decision to do something differently. Making the decision to become an excellent time manager is the first major step.

Program Your Mind

The mind is a powerful tthing and most of us take it for granted because we believe we are not incontrol. When indeed we are. We all have a mind of our own, capable of imagining life the way we want. For example, Once you have made the decision to become a highly productive person, there are a series of personal programming techniques that you can practice.

The first is to change your inner dialogue. Ninety-five percent of your emotions, and your eventual actions are determined by the way that you talk to yourself most of the time. Repeat to yourself, "I am well organized and highly productive." Whenever you feel overwhelmed with too much work, take a time-out and say to yourself, "I am well organized and highly productive."

Affirm over and over to yourself that "I am an excellent time manager." If people ask you about your time usage, tell them "I am an excellent time manager."

Whenever you say that "I am well organized," your subconscious accepts these words as a command and begins to motivate you to actually becoming well organized in your behaviors.

Visualize Yourself as Who You Want to Be

The second way to transform your behaviors is to visualize yourself as an excellent time manager. See yourself as organized, efficient, and in control of your life. Remember, the person you "see" on the inside is the person you will "be" on the outside.

If you are already a well-organized and highly productive person, how would you behave differently? What would be different from the way you behave today? Create a picture of yourself as calm, confident, highly efficient, more relaxed, and able to complete large amounts of work in a short period of time.

Imagine what a highly productive person will look like. Would the person's desk be clear and tidy? Would the person appear unhurried and unstressed? Create a clear mental picture of yourself as a person who is in control of his time and life.

Act "As If"

The third way to program yourself is to act "as if" you were already a good time manager. Think of yourself as being well organized in everything you do. If you were already excellent in time management, how would you behave? What would you be doing differently? With regard to your time and personal productivity, what would be different from the way you do things now? Interestingly enough, even if you do not think that you are a good time manager today, but nonetheless you pretend that you already are, these actions will generate a feeling of personal efficiency. You can actually change your actions, habits, and behavior when you "face it until you make it."

FINAL THOUGHTS

Building a 'tower of change,' we need to lay down the foundations first. You could also think of it as getting a toolkit for life (A toolkit comprises a set of tools that are used for achieving certain goals). First, put on the tool belt, then add into it one tool at a time. Eventually, you will have all the tools you need and know which tool to use for what job.

Life changes all the the time whether you like it or not. Time quickly moves on, we can either move with it or we can loose ourselves and fall. This is a very simple statement, a blunt assessment but it is really a good thing. There's no hero moment, just small steps towards feeling like everything is loosely together again. Getting your life together is not a one-off effort. So you need to inform yourself that you are willing to maximise your own potential to take advantage of the world. You can't jump from "I'm stupid" to "I'm brilliant" but you can move from "I'm stupid" to "there are many things I do well and some I do not so well." Keep it believable and positive.

Think about what a foundation is to a house - the strong base that supports the structure and body of the home. What happens if a house is built on a weak foundation or with no foundation at all?

What does this mean? Imagine that you are building a house. If you just start building, without properly preparing the site for the house, you might find that the house sags in places, that you've built it over an underground stream, or that it will fall down because of shifts in the ground.

Over time the house starts to fall apart and much work has to be done to save it. If nothing is done the house eventually collapses.

Your goals are like the house. Goals you pursue need to have a solid foundation upon which to build. Without that, they collapse. Even if you are able to achieve them, they may disappear because the foundation isn't there to keep the outcome solidly there.

How would you assess the quality of your foundation right now? Is it stable and sturdy or is it wobbly and weak? Do you even have one? A life built on a strong foundation can withstand a great deal of pressure but one built on a weak foundation (or none at all) will ultimately topple under pressure.

In order to have personal and small business growth you must have a strong foundation upon which you can build to become more and attract more.

When we want to strengthen our personal foundation what we really are saying is that we deserve and want more for ourselves.

BUILD YOUR PERSONAL FOUNDATION: The basis of starting on your foundations is essentially to clarify what you need to achieve with your life; how are you going to set these foundations up? And an element you need to consider is how long will the process take?

There are many areas within your foundations that you

need to look at; start by making a list of what you need as far as your life is concerned and work from there. Know yourself first. Know your attitudes, feelings, your skills, and mostly your goals and desires you want. These make up your personal power. When you feel good about who you are, then you are once again in control. Your outcomes from situations are your responsibility, you are not the victim. You can make better choices. Having personal power creates a mindset for success, whatever it may be.

What would happen if you lived your life by design rather than by default? What would happen if you took the time to choose what you wanted in life rather than letting life choose it for you? I am sure that many of you know people who appear to be living their lives on 'autopilot', rather than in control of their own personal destiny.

Accept the fact that you are not gifted with everything. All you can do about your life is try to be the best that you can be using the available resources in front of you. While you are still young, you have to know your strength and weaknesses. You have to be familiar with the things that you can do best. From there, start building your dreams using all the strong bricks as your foundation.

There is something that you are destined to do that no one else can do. A place that you are to fill, that no one else can fill! There is a way to jump off of the sinking ship of mediocrity.

Take a good hard look at you life right now and ask yourself:

"How is it possible for me to be successful if I am not in control of my own life?"

"If I am not the one in the driver's seat, then who or what is?"

Living your life in the driver's seat means that you know what you want and what is most important to you. You live a balanced and happy life filled with purpose and meaning. You have taken the time to create an authentic, vibrant and happy life, because if you don't take the time to choose what you want, life will choose it for you. You simply cannot be truly successful until you take back your control, and get back in the driver's seat of your life!

The way to get back into the driver's seat of your life is to create a life strategy. If you want to get the most out of your money you create a financial strategy. The same is true for your life. If you want to get the most out of your life you need to create a life strategy. The greater the detail of your strategy, the greater your experience of personal success.

A sound life strategy can be described as a house. The bottom foundation of your house is your personal foundation. The stronger it is, the less likely your house/life will crumble under stress. The four cornerstones of your house/life are:

- clarity of what your life is like now
- clarity of what you want your life to be
- cleaning up unfinished business from your past
- clarity of the beliefs and attitudes

The roof of your house is made up of the strategies that you set in place to build the life you desire and get you moving in the direction of your own personal success.

ACCEPT RESPONSIBILITY FOR YOUR ACTIONS: If you make a mistake, accept responsibility for it. You can be your biggest critic or your biggest supporter; the choice is up to you. Being fully responsible for your life will greatly determine how successful you will be in life.

Each time you refuse to take responsibility for your life you give your power away to circumstances or other people and as a result you disempower yourself. Accepting to take responsibility in all areas of your life will turn you into someone that creates his life rather than someone who is a victim of his environment. Acknowledging that you have a part of responsibility in everything in your life and that there is always ways for improvement will give you the right mindset to grow.

Cleanse your mind. Instead of falling victim to those negative thoughts, make a conscious effort to get rid of them. Promise yourself that you're not going to let some negativity define who you are. Remember, your entire demeanor is based on what you think!

Similar to the way a healthy diet can help your waist line, healthy thoughts can help your demeanor. If you truly want to take control of your life and be happier, you can't feed your mind negative thoughts. Instead, you have to understand you're in control of those thoughts - and let them go. If you dwell on it, the negativity and your complaining will never go away.

Cleanse your mind, purify your heart, heal your insecurities, heal your pain and you will start to see your life healing and you will begin to feel stronger. Something that is important to stress is, do not continue being around any and all abusive environments. Anything and anyone that takes you back to the cycle of abuse and the pain associated with it, remove yourself permanently. Don't keep going back to things and relationships that constantly brings up the pain of abuse for you and keeps you from moving forward. If those perpetuating the abuse wants to be in your life then they need to clean up their behaviour. Make sure you are not the one pushing them to change. They need to see that in themselves for themselves. Focus on you and you alone. Do not take on the burdens of others because it will only serve to crash you right back down to that weakened state.

CHANGE YOUR BELIEFS, CHANGE YOUR LIFE: As I've read once, our skills, talents, knowledge and abilities are directly influenced by our own personal beliefs. Where do our beliefs come from? They are passed on from our families, picked up from our friends, absorbed in from teachers, peers and society, or triggered by our experiences.

So what really holds us back is not the world, it is our belief of the limitations that are really self-imposed.

Underneath your life circumstances are your actions and underneath your actions are your choices. Underneath these are your beliefs; thoughts and messages strung together to create the foundation upon which you build your life. Beliefs are not good or bad, right or wrong. They just are and they either support you in life or they limit you. Just like the old saying goes, "if you believe you can, you can. If you believe you can't, you can't."

Hence, if we want to develop our potentials, we must first get past the limitations we have set for ourselves.

IT'S IN YOU: First of all you are unique. There is only one of you. No one else is like you. The only person standing in your way of changing your life is you. Your friends aren't stopping you. Your family isn't stopping you. Only you can motivate yourself to change your life.

Lacking trust in ourselves will create a discord in our lives. If we do not believe in ourselves then we will be led by the nose-ring by others who also do not trust or believe in themselves. Don't be a sheep that follows the herd. Stand apart from the crowd and forge your own path.

Others will certainly Believe in You, Motivate You, and Inspire You. However, you can't wait for or depend on external confidence injections. TRUE Confidence comes from within. YOU have to believe in YOU. This belief in YOU is fortified with the right combination of Self-Esteem, Personal Accountability, and Courage.

What is stopping you from becoming who you want to be? Your friends want you to succeed. Your family wants you to succeed. You want to succeed. There is no one around to hold you back except yourself and your own hesitation. .

Within that statement is the word "Can." You "can" do

it. Not you "will" do it. Though the statement implies that anything is within your grasp, there is still that small element of doubt - doubt that is entirely in your control. YOU can do it. Not someone else will do it for you. Not it will magically change without the slightest bit of effort. You can do whatever you want, but you can only turn that "can" into "will" if you are willing to commit to achieving those goals.

Be optimistic. Have an 'I can do' attitude. Set the ways in your life to be positive. Do not see situations as hopeless, remember you are in charge of your outcomes. Optimistic people are doers who focus on solutions to a problem. If they do not succeed the first time, they try until they do.

In order to move forward, we must have a mind shift. That shift begins with doing the work of being clear about who you are and who you want to be (or what you want your business or organization to become). Often what stops us from moving forward is that we are waiting for that perfect moment to work on ourselves. Here is the truth; (truth is defined as the real state of things), Time waits for no one.

None of us truly know how much time we really have. While we are waiting on the right time to get maximized, our life is passing us by. There will eventually come a moment when you will turn around and see that although time has passed, the dreams you have had for your life, business, ministry continue to live on within you.

So how do you move forward? You must get rid of "Stinking Thinking". This type of thinking is anything that is toxic to the dream or goal that you have in mind. Right now, make a conscious decision begin anew by getting in touch with the dreams and goals that you had for your life, the ones that you felt you could not do until:

- You had enough money
- You were married
- You get your life together
- Place your excuse here

These things are roadblocks and you must be aware of them and most importantly you must choose to get past them so that you can begin to live in your maximized life.

IF YOU DON'T FAIL THAT MEANS YOU ARE NOT EVEN TRYING: There are times when you would tell yourself that you couldn't do certain things so you don't even give it a try. But you'll be surprised that you can do these things as surely as anybody else can do only if you have decided to give it a try. You may encounter many defeats, but you must not be defeated. In fact, it may be necessary to encounter the defeats so you can know who you are, what you can rise from, and how you can still come out of it."

Failure truly is a humbling experience, but it is an excellent tutor. Everyone fails in life. At one point or another in your existence, you are going to fail. It is inevitable! If you want to succeed, double your failure rate "You cannot be successful without failure" and so forth.

You will not conquer what you never confront. Countries fought for their freedom, companies formed, inventions developed, promotions earned and athletes achieved all because they took a chance on a dream, failed many times in the process, and eventually succeeded. Founding father Benjamin Franklin never thought he failed, he just found many ways he did it wrong. Coach Vince Lombardi argued that he never lost a game, he just ran out of time.

The reason most people do not pursue their dreams is because they fear the idea of change. "Change is inevitable; growth is optional," Your situation will not begin to change until you do.

Fear has been acronymed False Evidence Appearing Real or Finding

Excuses And Running. Just as a soldier prepares for battle or an athlete prepares for a game, you must study your opponent in order to win. In order to conquer fear you must first understand what it really is. Fear is nothing more than a distressing emotion aroused by impending danger, whether the threat is real or imagined. An emotion is a feeling and your feelings are often unreliable. In short, fear is nothing more than an unreliable, stress-induced emotion. Can you think of an occasion(s) where you faced insurmountable odds only to overcome them victoriously? No matter how many times you were knocked down, you got back up and by sheer determination fought, scratched and clawed until you prevailed. The more fear you confront and conquer the greater courage you will possess."

Tough times do not last, but tough people like you do. Do

not let the minute details become a roadblock in your quest for success. One day you will be able to laugh when you look back on the adversities you face today. Many of us have lost our jobs, homes, autos, marriages, and financial independence, and much more. You may have faced some unbelievable obstacles, but remember someone, somewhere has it worse than you. One thing you can never let go of is HOPE (Have an Opportunistic Perspective Everyday). Always keep the mindset that problems are cleverly disguised opportunities and you must be ready to seize them. Faith in your todays will make sense in your tomorrows.

The best thing about failure is it is temporary, manageable and solvable. As a concept, failure on the way to success is a seemingly less threatening concept to our sense of well being rather than the concept of failure as the sum total of our efforts. It is therefore better to treat failure this way and cope with it adequately.

I encourage you to take another shot at the game of life; if you fail try, try again. Whenever you begin something new or start down a new path, you will experience a rush of emotions that could stop you in your tracks. Fear, anxiety, discomfort, self doubt, and procrastination will attempt to build a brick wall right in the middle of your path. These feelings may arrive and if you are aware of them, you will be able to raise your shield of defense and conquer them. As you proceed on your chartered course of change, you can use the following approaches to overcome the negative emotions that may arise: explore with a fun, curious, playful approach, go forward with unwavering self belief, be kind to yourself, proceed with courage, and be flexible with your master plan as required.

To be able to get past your limits, you must first take that one easy step. Once you discovered what you can do with just one try, you'll be excited and begin to think what else you're capable of. Soon, you'll be getting way beyond limit after limit after limit. Eventually, you have no limits anymore and you'll find yourself on the way to success.

Always remember it's okay to make mistakes. As long as we own up to them and learn from these mistakes. Conscious effort to change what is not working in your life.

COMMIT TO IT: The quality of a person's life is in direct proportion to their commitment to excellence, regardless of their chosen field of endeavor. - Vince Lombardi

Setting goals and having a plan is one thing; but without action, it all becomes wishful thinking.

Thomas Edison had a vision for many years that he would discover a bulb. He tried for so many years, with no luck. However, he was committed to his goal and knew that he will succeed some day and he did. Let me ask you, are you committed to succeed? Are you committed to challenge all the obstacles to achieve your goals?

The secret to achieving your goals is commitment - something which is straightforward but not always easy to do. All you need to do is commit to putting your goals into action. It's that simple.

Without that absolute commitment then your goals are

nothing more than empty promises and false hopes. There will be no actual plan of action to achieve your goals.

However, when you truly commit yourself to achieving your goals you redefine the meaning of impossible. "All things are possible until they are proved impossible - and even the impossible may only be so, as of now." - Pearl S. Buck

Now it's time to take seriously your efforts to succeed. Success takes commitment. Success takes time. To experience success in any area of your life, you have to be able to push past life's road blocks. Commit to not quit! Focus your thoughts on the prize you seek, not the challenges.

One of my favorite remedies for the tough times is saying aloud, "I will not be defeated and I will not quit." Repeat as needed.

Commitment requires discipline. If you've made a commitment - to yourself or someone else, use discipline to fulfill that promise. Not only will it help you reach your goals, you'll feel better about yourself in the process.

Commitment is aided by routine. Commit to spending a certain amount of time each day on your goal or to focus on the project at a specific time each day. Use your most creative time of day to work on your greatest challenges. For some, that's early morning, before the day's events interfere. Some are most creative and energetic in the afternoon. Others prefer the quiet of evening. Whatever works for you, if you'll make it a routine, it will soon become a habit. The habit of commitment will carry you to success.

Commitment requires tough decisions. I've always told my

daughter, "If you spend it there, you won't have it to spend somewhere else". The same is true with your time, talents, energy. Use your internal check list (peace) to decide where to commit yourself. What goals are most important for your wellbeing? Find ways to say "NO" to the things and people who drain you of your energy and efforts.

Commit yourself to achieving your goals, and be ready to experience the joy that comes from reaching the objectives you have set out for yourself.

However, there is one other secret ingredient to achieving your goals. It is desire. You have to truly want your goal. Without desire you will not be motivated to achieve your goal. You have to have a burning passion for it otherwise you will never commit to achieving it. "Desire is the key to motivation, but its determination and commitment to an unrelenting pursuit of your goal - a commitment to excellence - that will enable you to attain the success you seek." - Mario Andretti

What goal will you irrevocably commit to achieving? "To get what you want in life you must develop the ability to think in the way that will support your goals and dreams."

When we're in hot pursuit of our dreams and goals it can feel effortless, but when enthusiasm wanes so can our motivation. Sometimes we falsely believe that our dream or goal is the problem, but truthfully what we need are stronger motivation muscles. We need a motivated mindset. We have to become mindful to do those things that will create an actual mind shift and then we can be assured that our motivation mojo will remain available no matter what.

Pursue your dreams; conquer your goals; and recover all that you have wasted by allowing fear to paralyze you. Having fear condones inaction; having faith condemns it.

The first step is always the biggest, but do not let it prevent you from starting on this new exciting journey. Open one door. Just open it and peak in if that is where you want to start. You don't have to step in if you choose not to and you can even step in and change your mind and step back out closing the door behind you. The goal here is to begin, be curious, explore, and step forward. It is important we spend time being positive about today. We must choose to be involved in the moments our life.

So really the answer to "What is stopping you?" is YOU! Today you can take the first small step towards great changes! First, just decide whether you want to become the very best you can and to achieve your true potential. Be brave, be bold, be persistent! You navigate the life you want to live — it all starts with you. Get your S.H.I.T together.

DAILY POSITIVE AFFIRMATIONS

I use affirmations to help with my situations and negative thoughts. Many of us have negative thoughts sometimes, and even frequently. When we think negatively our confidence, frame of mind and outlook can become negative too. We talk ourselves into believing that we're not good enough and it effects our personal lives. If we intentionally do the opposite and use positive thoughts about ourselves, the effect can be just as powerful. Affirmations are positive statements that can help you overcome self defeating and negative thoughts.

The power of affirmations lies in repeating them daily to yourself. As well as repeating them when you engage in negative thoughts or situations that you want to overcome. Affirmations work best when you visualize the change you like to see. They help reprogram your subconscious mind, encouraging you to believe in yourself and help create the reality you want. Otherwise, attracting whatever it is that you desire. I used this very list on the start of my self care journey every morning and still use them today. You too can!

I forgive myself for not being perfect because I know I'm human.
I accept what I cannot change.
I make the best of every situation

I have control over my thoughts, feelings and choices.

I know, accept and am true to myself.

I give myself the care and attention I deserve.

I trust that I am on the right path.

I am at peace with who I am as a person.

I give myself permission to do what's right for me.

I am proud of myself, I choose myself.

I am doing my best.

I trust in my ability to survive and thrive through obstacles.

I value my time and input.

I am so grateful to be alive.

I am blessed.

I am supported.

I am loved.

I am enough.

I am strong.

I am beautiful.

Making the most of affirmations on a daily base can uplift, motivate and inspire you. Feel free to create your own checklist-affirmations that best suits your needs. Keep in mind you are what you think. Keep it together!

ABOUT THE AUTHOR

Crystal Rose is a mother, health care professional and aspiring Entrepreneur. She's focused and driven to help bring awareness to others when it comes to self care after experiencing her lack of self care. It was then she found her true purpose for wanting to help others achieve their goals for coping with stress, anxiety and depression. She is currently building a self care brand, 'Rose Wurks'. For more information you can visit www.rosewurks. com . This is her first book.

Printed in the United States
By Bookmasters